The A.I. Revolution. Navigating the future of Artificial Intelligence

Arthur Crandon LL.B (Hons.) M.A.

Unlock the mysteries of tomorrow with *The A.I. Revolution: Navigating the Future of Artificial Intelligence.* Discover how AI reshapes industries, transforms societies, and redefines humanity's role. This book offers insights, challenges, and opportunities for thriving in a rapidly evolving world. Your guide to understanding and harnessing the power of AI.

CONTENTS

Step into the future with *The A.I. Revolution: Navigating the Future of Artificial Intelligence.*

This groundbreaking book explores AI's potential, challenges, and impact on our lives. From ethical dilemmas to innovation opportunities, uncover the tools you need to thrive in a world where technology and humanity intersect.

1 INTRODUCTION TO AI

What Is AI?

Artificial Intelligence, or AI, is not just a buzzword; it's a transformative force reshaping how we live, work, and interact with the world. At its core, AI refers to machines or software that mimic human intelligence to perform tasks like learning, reasoning, problem-solving, and decision-making. What makes AI unique is its ability to improve over time, becoming smarter and more efficient as it processes data.

Key Concepts in AI:

1. **Machine Learning (ML):** A subset of AI where algorithms learn from data to make predictions or decisions. ML powers everything from spam filters to medical diagnostics.

2. **Deep Learning:** A more advanced form of ML that uses artificial neural networks to mimic the human brain. Deep learning is behind breakthroughs in image recognition, language processing, and autonomous vehicles.

3. **Neural Networks:** Modeled after the human brain, these interconnected nodes (neurons) process information in layers to recognize patterns and make decisions.

4. **Natural Language Processing (NLP):** The technology enabling machines to understand, interpret, and generate human language. Applications include virtual assistants like Siri and chatbots.

5. **Generative AI:** A cutting-edge development where AI creates original content—be it text, images, music, or code—based on the data it's trained on.

These components come together to form the backbone of AI systems that are increasingly embedded in our daily lives.

A Brief History of AI: From Alan Turing to GPT-4 and Beyond

The story of AI is one of human ingenuity, marked by both breakthroughs and setbacks. It began in 1950 when Alan Turing, the father of computer science, posed the famous question: "Can machines think?" His Turing Test laid the foundation for measuring a machine's ability to exhibit intelligent behavior indistinguishable from that of a human.

Key Milestones in AI History:

- **1956:** The term "Artificial Intelligence" was coined at the Dartmouth Conference, marking the birth of AI as a field of study.

- **1960s-70s:** Early successes included programs that could solve math problems and play chess, but the field struggled due to limited computing power.

- **1980s:** The rise of "expert systems" brought AI into businesses, enabling machines to simulate human decision-making in specific domains.

- **1997:** IBM's Deep Blue defeated chess grandmaster Garry Kasparov, proving that

3

machines could outthink humans in specific tasks.

- **2011:** IBM's Watson won *Jeopardy!* by mastering natural language processing and vast data analysis.

- **2016:** Google DeepMind's AlphaGo beat the world champion in the ancient game of Go, a feat previously thought impossible for machines.

- **2023:** OpenAI's GPT-4 showcased the potential of generative AI, revolutionizing industries from content creation to coding.

The journey from Turing's theoretical question to today's AI breakthroughs underscores humanity's relentless pursuit of innovation.

Why AI Matters Now

AI has evolved from a futuristic concept to a pervasive force influencing nearly every aspect of modern life. What sets this moment apart is the sheer scale and speed at which AI is advancing, transforming industries and societies alike.

The Explosion of AI Applications

AI is no longer confined to research labs or tech giants—it's everywhere:

- In your pocket: Virtual assistants like Siri and Google Assistant answer questions, schedule tasks, and even tell jokes.

- At work: AI powers predictive analytics in business, automates tedious tasks, and helps companies make data-driven decisions.

- In healthcare: AI assists in diagnosing diseases, identifying drug candidates, and improving patient care.

- In transportation: Autonomous vehicles, traffic optimization, and ride-sharing algorithms rely on AI to function seamlessly.

This rapid integration makes AI indispensable, but it also raises questions about its broader implications.

AI's Role in Addressing Global Challenges

AI's potential to solve complex problems is one of its most exciting prospects. For example:

- **Climate Change:** AI analyzes vast datasets to predict weather patterns, optimize energy usage, and design sustainable solutions.

- **Healthcare Crises:** During the COVID-19 pandemic, AI was instrumental in vaccine development and tracking the virus's spread.

- **Global Hunger:** AI enhances agricultural productivity through precision farming, reducing waste, and increasing yields.

The Flip Side: AI's Risks

While AI holds immense promise, it also exacerbates challenges:

- **Job Displacement:** Automation threatens to replace millions of jobs, particularly in manufacturing, retail, and transportation.

- **Bias and Inequality:** AI systems can reinforce societal biases, as seen in facial recognition technologies that perform poorly on minority groups.

- **Privacy Concerns:** AI-driven surveillance raises ethical questions about individual rights in an increasingly interconnected world.

Expanding the Discussion: Additional Topics for the Introduction

1. **The Philosophical Debate: Can Machines Truly Think?**

   Discuss the ongoing philosophical debate about whether machines can achieve consciousness or if they will always remain tools designed by humans. What are the ethical implications if AI becomes indistinguishable from human thought?

2. **The Democratization of AI**
   Explain how AI is becoming more accessible. Tools like ChatGPT or Canva's AI features allow individuals and small businesses to leverage AI without needing deep technical knowledge.

3. **The Race for AI Supremacy**
Highlight the geopolitical implications of AI, including the competition between nations like the U.S. and China to dominate this critical technology. How does this race affect global power dynamics?

4. **AI in Pop Culture: Vision vs. Reality**
Explore how AI is portrayed in films and books—from dystopian tales like *The Terminator* to hopeful visions like *Her*. Compare these narratives to the real-world capabilities and challenges of AI.

Conclusion

AI is no longer the realm of science fiction—it's here, shaping the present and defining the future. As we embark on this journey through the AI revolution, it's crucial to understand not just what AI is but why it matters now more than ever. This book will unpack the opportunities, risks, and ethical dilemmas of AI, equipping readers to navigate an era where artificial intelligence is poised to be one of the most transformative forces in human history.

Insert chapter one text here. Insert chapter one text here. Insert chapter one text here. Insert chapter one text here.

2 THE AI ECOSYSTEM

Players, Platforms, and Innovations

The world of artificial intelligence is a dynamic ecosystem driven by influential companies, cutting-edge technologies, and intense global competition. To understand the AI revolution, we must explore the key players leading innovation, the technologies shaping our future, and the geopolitical landscape that defines AI's role in the 21st century.

Key Innovators and Companies

AI development is spearheaded by a mix of tech giants, startups, and academic institutions. These entities are pushing the boundaries of what

AI can achieve, competing fiercely while occasionally collaborating to drive innovation.

1. OpenAI

- **Role in AI Innovation:** OpenAI has become synonymous with breakthroughs in generative AI, creating tools like GPT-4 and DALL-E. These platforms have redefined natural language processing (NLP) and content creation, making AI accessible to businesses and individuals alike.

- **Vision:** OpenAI's mission to ensure that artificial general intelligence (AGI) benefits all of humanity guides its projects, balancing technological progress with ethical considerations.

2. Google DeepMind

- **Achievements:** DeepMind's AlphaGo was a watershed moment, showcasing AI's ability to master complex tasks. The company continues to excel in applying AI to solve scientific problems, such as predicting protein structures with AlphaFold.

- **Focus Areas:** DeepMind is a leader in reinforcement learning and integrating AI into healthcare, gaming, and scientific research.

3. Microsoft

- **AI Integration:** Microsoft has embedded AI across its product ecosystem, from Azure's cloud-based AI services to AI-enhanced tools in Office 365.

- **Partnerships:** Its investment in OpenAI underscores its commitment to leading the AI race. With integrations like GPT-powered Copilot in Office products, Microsoft brings generative AI to millions of users.

4. Amazon

- **AI in E-commerce:** Amazon uses AI extensively in its recommendation algorithms, logistics optimization, and customer service chatbots.

- **AWS Dominance:** Amazon Web Services (AWS) offers AI and machine learning tools that power businesses globally, cementing Amazon's influence in enterprise AI.

5. Tesla

- **Autonomous Vehicles:** Tesla's AI-driven advancements in self-driving technology position it as a leader in AI applications for transportation.

- **Innovation Hubs:** With its Dojo supercomputer and expertise in neural networks, Tesla aims to revolutionize autonomous systems and robotics.

6. NVIDIA

- **Hardware Backbone:** NVIDIA's GPUs are the backbone of AI research and deployment, providing the computational power needed for training complex models.

- **Emerging Influence:** The company's work in AI frameworks, such as CUDA and TensorRT, enables developers worldwide to innovate.

Other Players to Watch:

- **IBM:** Known for its AI platform Watson, which specializes in enterprise solutions.

- **Meta:** Focused on AI for social media, content moderation, and metaverse applications.

- **Startups:** Companies like Anthropic and Cohere are emerging challengers in the generative AI space.

Emerging Technologies

AI's rapid evolution is fueled by breakthroughs in several foundational and cutting-edge technologies. These innovations are shaping the way machines interact with humans and the world.

1. **Natural Language Processing (NLP)**

- **Definition:** NLP enables machines to understand, interpret, and generate human language.

- **Applications:** ChatGPT and translation tools like Google Translate exemplify NLP's potential in communication, content creation, and customer service.

2. Computer Vision

- **Capabilities:** AI-powered systems that interpret and analyze visual data are transforming industries like healthcare (medical imaging) and retail (visual search).

- **Examples:** Facial recognition, object detection, and augmented reality applications.

3. Generative AI

- **Definition:** Generative AI creates new content, from text and images to music and videos, based on patterns learned from data.

- **Impact:** Tools like DALL-E and MidJourney are revolutionizing art and design, while generative models like GPT are reshaping writing, coding, and customer interactions.

4. Robotics and Autonomous Systems

- **Applications:** AI-driven robots are enhancing manufacturing, logistics, and healthcare. Autonomous drones and vehicles are redefining transportation and delivery systems.

5. Ethical and Explainable AI

- **Focus:** As AI becomes more pervasive, ensuring transparency and fairness in decision-making is a critical research area.

- **Examples:** Developing models that can explain their outputs to humans, reducing bias in AI systems.

6. Advanced AI Training Models

- **Trends:** Transformer models, reinforcement learning, and unsupervised learning are driving AI's ability to learn from less data and achieve higher accuracy.

Global Landscape

The AI revolution is a global phenomenon, with innovation hubs emerging across the world. Each region brings unique strengths and challenges to the development and deployment of AI.

1. United States

- **Leadership Role:** Home to Silicon Valley, the U.S. remains the epicenter of AI innovation. Companies like Google, Microsoft, and OpenAI lead the charge, backed by significant government and venture capital investment.

- **Challenges:** Balancing innovation with regulatory oversight and addressing ethical concerns.

2. China

- **Rapid Growth:** With state-backed initiatives, China aims to be the global leader in AI by 2030. Companies like Baidu, Tencent, and Alibaba dominate AI research, particularly in facial recognition and e-commerce.

- **Focus Areas:** Surveillance, smart cities, and autonomous technologies.

- **Global Impact:** China's investments in AI extend to Africa, Southeast Asia, and Europe, creating strategic alliances.

3. European Union

- **Ethical Leadership:** The EU prioritizes ethical AI development, focusing on privacy, accountability, and bias mitigation.

- **Regulatory Frameworks:** The AI Act aims to set global standards for responsible AI deployment.

4. Emerging Markets

- **India:** Leveraging its tech talent, India focuses on AI for agriculture, healthcare, and education.

- **Africa:** AI initiatives in Africa address local challenges, such as resource allocation and disease tracking.

- **Latin America:** Startups in Brazil and Mexico are driving AI adoption in fintech and agriculture.

International Collaborations and Rivalries Collaborations:

- AI research transcends borders, with collaborations between academia, industry, and governments.

- Examples: Partnerships like the Global Partnership on Artificial Intelligence (GPAI) and cross-border research initiatives.

Rivalries:

- The U.S.-China AI rivalry dominates the global landscape, influencing trade, security, and innovation.

- Concerns about "AI nationalism" risk creating fragmented ecosystems, limiting the potential for shared progress.

The Role of Global Standards:

Efforts to create international agreements on AI ethics and governance are critical to preventing misuse and ensuring equitable benefits.

Conclusion

The AI ecosystem is a complex web of innovation, competition, and collaboration. With major players leading groundbreaking advancements, emerging technologies transforming industries, and global rivalries shaping the future, the AI revolution is poised to redefine how humanity interacts with technology. Understanding this ecosystem is key to navigating the challenges and opportunities of artificial intelligence in the modern world.

3 THE POST PANDEMIC WORLD

How COVID-19 Reshaped Society

The COVID-19 pandemic was more than a global health crisis—it was a seismic event that altered the fabric of society. Its effects ripple across healthcare, education, work culture, and mental health, reshaping how we live, connect, and interact with the world. This chapter delves into the long-term impacts of the pandemic, weaving personal narratives, expert analyses, and a broader societal perspective to paint a comprehensive picture of its enduring legacy.

Healthcare: From Crisis to Transformation

COVID-19 tested healthcare systems worldwide, exposing vulnerabilities while accelerating innovation.

1. Strengthened Public Health Infrastructure

- **Pandemic Preparedness:** Countries are investing in early detection systems and stockpiles of medical supplies to mitigate future crises.

- **Global Collaboration:** Initiatives like the COVAX program highlighted the importance of equitable vaccine distribution, though disparities persist.

2. Telemedicine Revolution

- **Accessibility and Convenience:** Virtual consultations became mainstream, breaking down geographical barriers to care.

- **Challenges:** Patients and providers grappled with technology adoption, raising questions about access for underserved populations.

3. Mental Health Awareness

- **Impact of Isolation:** The pandemic brought mental health to the forefront, with widespread anxiety, depression, and burnout leading to increased demand for services.

- **Cultural Shift:** Societies began destigmatizing mental health, prompting governments and organizations to invest in support programs.

4. Vaccine Development Milestone

- **mRNA Technology:** The rapid development of vaccines using mRNA technology has implications far beyond COVID-19, paving the way for advances in treating cancer and other diseases.

Education: A Digital Revolution

The pandemic forced an abrupt shift to remote learning, reshaping education in ways that will endure.

1. Rise of Online Learning

- **Digital Transformation:** Schools and universities adapted to virtual platforms, accelerating the adoption of digital tools.

- **Access and Inequality:** The digital divide became glaringly apparent, with underserved students struggling to keep up due to lack of resources.

2. Hybrid Learning Models

- **Blended Approaches:** Institutions now embrace hybrid learning models, combining in-person and online experiences to offer flexibility.

- **Student Engagement:** While technology offered opportunities, educators faced challenges in maintaining engagement and assessing learning outcomes.

3. Parental Involvement

- **Home as a Classroom:** Parents took on new roles as facilitators of their children's education, fostering greater appreciation for teachers while highlighting the need for better work-life balance.

4. Lifelong Learning Surge

- **Upskilling and Reskilling:** Adults turned to online platforms like Coursera and Khan Academy to gain new skills, reflecting a cultural shift toward continuous education in a rapidly changing job market.

Work Culture: Redefining Productivity

The pandemic redefined how, where, and why we work, leaving a lasting impact on workplace norms and values.

1. Remote Work Revolution

- **Flexibility as Norm:** Remote work, once a niche arrangement, became mainstream, with many companies adopting permanent or hybrid models.

- **Tech Integration:** Tools like Zoom, Microsoft Teams, and Slack revolutionized collaboration but also raised concerns about digital fatigue.

2. Shift in Workforce Priorities

- **The Great Resignation:** Employees reevaluated priorities, leading to mass resignations and a focus on work-life balance.

- **Well-being at Work:** Employers now prioritize mental health initiatives, flexible schedules, and empathetic leadership.

3. Automation and AI Acceleration

- **Job Displacement:** The pandemic spurred adoption of AI and automation, streamlining operations but raising concerns about job loss.

- **New Roles:** As old jobs disappeared, roles in tech, remote facilitation, and logistics emerged.

4. Globalization vs. Localization

- **Distributed Teams:** Companies embraced global talent pools, hiring employees regardless of location.

- **Resilience through Localization:** Simultaneously, businesses reconsidered supply chains, emphasizing local production to mitigate risks.

Mental Health: A Societal Awakening

The pandemic left an indelible mark on mental health, transforming how individuals and societies approach emotional well-being.

1. The Toll of Isolation

- **Increased Loneliness:** Prolonged lockdowns amplified feelings of loneliness and disconnection, especially among the elderly and young adults.

- **Coping Mechanisms:** People turned to online communities, mindfulness apps, and teletherapy to manage stress.

2. Burnout Epidemic

- **Work-Life Blurring:** Remote work blurred boundaries, leading to an epidemic of burnout as individuals struggled to disconnect.

- **Employer Response:** Organizations began offering mental health days, counseling services, and flexible work arrangements.

3. Focus on Children and Teens

- **Impact of School Closures:** Interrupted education and limited social interaction left a generation grappling with anxiety and developmental delays.

- **Support Systems:** Schools and parents are increasingly prioritizing mental health resources to address these challenges.

4. Cultural Shifts in Stigma

- **Normalization of Therapy:** The pandemic made therapy more accessible and less stigmatized, with public figures advocating for mental health awareness.

Personal Narratives and Expert Insights

1. Stories from the Frontlines

- **Healthcare Workers:** Firsthand accounts from doctors, nurses, and paramedics who faced unprecedented challenges.

- **Educators and Parents:** Stories of resilience and adaptation as families navigated remote learning.

2. Expert Analyses

- **Economists:** Assessing the pandemic's long-term impact on global economies.

- **Psychologists:** Insights into collective trauma and post-pandemic mental health recovery.

- **Sociologists:** How the pandemic reshaped communities and interpersonal relationships.

Global Legacy of the Pandemic

1. Geopolitical Shifts

- **Health Diplomacy:** Nations that excelled in managing the pandemic gained soft power, while others faced criticism.

- **Global Cooperation:** The pandemic underscored the importance of multilateral efforts to address shared challenges.

2. Preparedness for Future Crises

- **Lessons Learned:** Investments in healthcare, education, and crisis management ensure societies are better equipped for future emergencies.

3. Cultural and Behavioral Changes

- **Adoption of Technology:** The normalization of digital interactions reshapes how we socialize, shop, and work.

- **Resilience and Adaptation:** Communities learned to innovate and adapt, proving humanity's capacity for resilience in the face of adversity.

Conclusion: A New Normal

COVID-19 was a defining event of the 21st century, and its legacy will continue to shape our world for years to come. From healthcare innovations to cultural transformations, the pandemic forced societies to confront vulnerabilities while sparking progress in unexpected ways. As we reflect on the lessons learned, we must also consider the opportunities to build a more equitable, connected, and resilient world. Through personal narratives, expert insights, and analysis, this book offers a roadmap to understanding the profound ways COVID-19 reshaped society.

4 AI'S TRANSFORMATIVE ROLE

AI's Transformative Role in Industries

Artificial Intelligence (AI) is reshaping industries, driving innovation, and solving challenges once thought insurmountable. Its applications span from life-saving healthcare breakthroughs to redefining how we learn, work, and entertain ourselves. In this chapter, we explore the transformative role of AI across key sectors, highlighting success stories, challenges, and emerging opportunities.

Healthcare: Revolutionizing Patient Care

AI's integration into healthcare is nothing short of revolutionary, enabling faster diagnoses, personalized treatments, and improved patient outcomes.

1. Diagnostics

- **Precision and Speed:** AI-powered tools analyze medical images, such as X-rays and MRIs, with remarkable accuracy, often detecting conditions like cancer or fractures faster than human radiologists.

- **Examples:** Google Health's AI model for breast cancer detection outperforms traditional methods, reducing false positives and missed diagnoses.

2. Drug Discovery

- **Accelerating Innovation:** AI shortens drug development timelines by identifying potential compounds, predicting outcomes, and analyzing massive datasets.

- **Success Story:** During the COVID-19 pandemic, AI expedited vaccine development by modeling protein structures and identifying potential targets.

3. Personalized Medicine

- **Tailored Treatments:** AI analyzes genetic data and patient history to recommend customized treatment plans.

- **Examples:** IBM Watson Health assists oncologists in creating targeted cancer therapies based on individual biomarkers.

4. Telemedicine

- **Remote Care:** AI chatbots and virtual assistants enhance telemedicine platforms, offering preliminary diagnoses and triaging patients.

- **Challenges:** Ensuring data privacy and maintaining a human touch in virtual interactions remain key concerns.

Finance: Transforming Risk Management and Investment

AI has become a cornerstone of modern finance, improving efficiency and reducing risks in a highly dynamic sector.

1. Fraud Detection

- **Real-Time Analysis:** AI systems monitor transactions for unusual patterns, flagging potential fraud in seconds.

- **Example:** PayPal uses AI algorithms to detect fraudulent activities across millions of transactions daily.

2. Algorithmic Trading

- **Market Insights:** AI-driven trading platforms analyze market trends, optimize investment strategies, and execute trades at lightning speed.

- **Advantage:** These systems often outperform human traders by reacting to micro-second fluctuations in the market.

3. Robo-Advisors

- **Democratizing Investment:** Platforms like Betterment and Wealthfront use AI to provide personalized financial advice and portfolio management, making investing accessible to the average consumer.

- **Challenges:** Balancing cost-efficiency with personalized service and managing risk during market volatility.

Education: Personalizing the Learning Experience

AI is transforming education by making learning more accessible, adaptive, and engaging for students of all ages.

1. Adaptive Learning Platforms

- **Customized Curriculums:** AI-driven platforms like DreamBox and Khan Academy adjust content and difficulty based on a student's performance, ensuring personalized learning.

- **Impact:** Students who struggle in traditional settings can thrive with tailored support.

2. AI Tutors

- **24/7 Assistance:** Virtual tutors powered by AI help students with homework, language learning, and test preparation.

- **Example:** Duolingo's AI features adapt lessons to individual progress, improving language acquisition.

3. Accessibility Improvements

- **Breaking Barriers:** AI tools like real-time transcription, sign language translation, and text-to-speech technology make education more inclusive for students with disabilities.

- **Success Story:** Microsoft's Seeing AI app helps visually impaired students navigate written content and their environment.

Transportation: The Path to Autonomy

AI is driving the future of transportation, making travel safer, smarter, and more efficient.

1. Autonomous Vehicles

- **Self-Driving Cars:** Companies like Tesla, Waymo, and GM Cruise are at the forefront of creating AI-powered vehicles capable of navigating complex traffic scenarios.

- **Challenges:** Ensuring safety, managing ethical dilemmas (e.g., accident decision-making), and addressing regulatory hurdles.

2. Traffic Optimization

- **Smarter Cities:** AI systems analyze traffic patterns to reduce congestion, optimize traffic lights, and improve public transportation schedules.

- **Example:** Singapore's AI-driven traffic management system significantly reduces commute times.

3. Drones and Delivery

- **Logistics Revolution:** AI-powered drones and robots are transforming last-mile delivery, particularly in rural and hard-to-reach areas.

-

- **Example:** Amazon's Prime Air program aims to make drone deliveries mainstream.

Entertainment and Media: Creativity Meets Technology

AI is redefining creativity, generating art, music, and stories while raising ethical and artistic questions.

1. AI-Generated Art and Music

- **Creative Collaborations:** Platforms like OpenAI's DALL-E and AIVA create stunning visuals and compositions, blending human input with AI creativity.

- **Implications:** While expanding creative possibilities, these tools challenge traditional notions of authorship and originality.

2. Writing and Content Creation

- **Automated Creativity:** AI tools like ChatGPT assist writers in generating articles, scripts, and novels, making content creation faster and more efficient.

- **Success Story:** Several AI-written books and music albums have gained public acclaim, showcasing the potential of machine creativity.

3. Deepfakes and Synthetic Media

- **The Double-Edged Sword:** AI can create hyper-realistic videos and audio, enabling innovative storytelling but also fueling misinformation and ethical dilemmas.

- **Example:** Deepfake videos of public figures raise concerns about political manipulation and trust.

Emerging Opportunities and Challenges

1. Industry Convergence

AI blurs boundaries between industries, creating synergies that unlock new possibilities. For example, AI in healthcare can integrate with AI in finance to improve medical billing accuracy and streamline payments.

2. Workforce Transformation

AI's integration across sectors creates demand for skilled professionals in AI development, data analysis, and ethics, while also threatening job displacement in certain roles.

3. Ethical Considerations

- **Bias and Fairness:** Ensuring AI systems operate without reinforcing societal biases is a critical challenge.

- **Regulation and Accountability:** Governments and industries must collaborate to set standards for AI use across sectors.

Conclusion

From diagnosing diseases and optimizing supply chains to creating art and shaping cities, AI is transforming industries at an unprecedented pace. While the benefits are immense, challenges such as ethical dilemmas, job displacement, and accessibility must be addressed to ensure AI serves humanity equitably. The next chapter of AI's evolution depends on how society chooses to balance innovation with responsibility, making it one of the most exciting pivotal eras in history.

5. Ethical Dilemmas and Risks

As artificial intelligence (AI) integrates into every facet of our lives, it brings with it a host of ethical dilemmas and risks that challenge societal norms, laws, and values. While the promise of AI is immense, these challenges must be addressed to ensure the technology serves humanity equitably and responsibly. In this chapter, we explore the most pressing ethical issues surrounding AI, offering real-world examples, critical analysis, and potential solutions.

Bias and Discrimination

AI systems are only as unbiased as the data they are trained on, and biases—whether unintentional or systemic—can lead to harmful consequences.

1. Examples of Algorithmic Bias

- **Facial Recognition Technology:** Studies show that facial recognition algorithms often struggle to identify individuals with darker skin tones, leading to wrongful arrests and surveillance targeting.

- **Hiring Algorithms:** AI systems used by companies like Amazon have historically favored male candidates because they were trained on past hiring data that reflected gender biases.

2. Societal Impact

- **Inequality Reinforcement:** Bias in AI can perpetuate and amplify existing inequalities, such as racial or gender disparities.

- **Loss of Trust:** Public faith in AI diminishes when systems consistently exhibit bias, potentially slowing adoption of otherwise beneficial technologies.

3. Addressing the Problem

- **Diverse Training Data:** Companies must ensure datasets are representative of diverse populations.

- **Algorithm Audits:** Regularly assessing AI systems for bias helps identify and mitigate discriminatory outcomes.

- **Inclusive Development:** Encouraging diverse teams in AI development fosters greater awareness of potential biases.

Privacy Concerns

AI's reliance on vast amounts of data raises questions about privacy, consent, and the balance between innovation and personal freedoms.

1. Data Collection and Surveillance

- **Ubiquity of Data:** AI systems like recommendation engines and voice assistants collect data continuously, often without explicit user consent.

- **Surveillance States:** Countries like China leverage AI for mass surveillance, using facial recognition and predictive algorithms to monitor and control populations.

2. The Right to Anonymity

- **Erosion of Privacy:** AI systems can de-anonymize data, exposing sensitive information about individuals.

- **Ethical Concerns:** Where should the line be drawn between public safety and individual privacy?

3. Solutions and Safeguards

- **Data Minimization:** Companies should collect only the data necessary for specific functions.

- **Stronger Regulations:** Policies like the EU's General Data Protection Regulation (GDPR) provide a framework for protecting personal data.

- **User Control:** Transparent systems that allow users to opt-in or opt-out of data collection empower individuals.

Job Displacement

AI's efficiency and cost-effectiveness make it an attractive alternative to human labor, but automation threatens to displace millions of jobs across industries.

1. Affected Industries

- **Manufacturing:** Robotics and AI have automated assembly lines, reducing the need for human workers.

- **Retail:** Automated checkout systems and inventory management are replacing cashiers and stock clerks.

- **Transportation:** Autonomous vehicles threaten jobs in trucking, delivery, and public transit.

2. Societal Implications

- **Economic Inequality:** Job displacement can exacerbate income disparities, particularly for low-skill workers.

- **Social Unrest:** Communities reliant on traditional industries may face economic decline and rising unemployment.

3. Strategies for Workforce Adaptation

- **Upskilling and Reskilling:** Governments and companies should invest in training programs to help workers transition into AI-driven industries.

- **Universal Basic Income (UBI):** UBI is increasingly discussed as a potential safety net for workers displaced by automation.

- **Human-AI Collaboration:** Designing roles where AI assists human workers rather than replacing them can create new opportunities.

AI in Warfare

The use of AI in military applications raises ethical concerns about the automation of life-and-death decisions.

1. Autonomous Weapons

- **Definition:** AI-powered systems, such as drones and robots, capable of identifying and engaging targets without human intervention.

- **Risks:** Autonomous weapons could misidentify targets, causing civilian casualties and escalating conflicts.

2. Ethical Dilemmas

- **Accountability:** Who is responsible when an autonomous weapon causes unintended harm—the developer, operator, or manufacturer?

- **Arms Race:** The development of AI-powered weapons risks triggering a global arms race, increasing the likelihood of conflict.

3. Preventative Measures

- **International Agreements:** Advocating for treaties that ban or regulate the use of autonomous weapons.

- **Human Oversight:** Ensuring humans remain in control of critical decision-making processes.

Misinformation and Manipulation

AI's ability to generate convincing fake content poses significant challenges to truth and trust in the digital age.

1. Deepfakes

- **Definition:** AI-generated videos or audio that convincingly mimic real people, often used maliciously to spread misinformation or harm reputations.

- **Real-World Examples:** Deepfake videos of public figures have been used to manipulate elections and spread false narratives.

2. Fake News Amplification

- **Role of AI:** Social media algorithms amplify sensationalist or misleading content to maximize engagement, fueling misinformation.

- **Impact:** False information can influence elections, incite violence, and undermine public trust in institutions.

3. Combating Misinformation

- **AI for Good:** AI tools can detect and flag fake content before it spreads widely.

- **Media Literacy:** Educating the public to critically evaluate online content can reduce the impact of misinformation.

- **Regulatory Oversight:** Governments and platforms must collaborate to create policies addressing the spread of AI-generated misinformation.

Emerging Ethical Concerns

1. AI Ownership and Accessibility

- **Concentration of Power:** Control over advanced AI systems is often concentrated among a few tech giants, raising concerns about monopolies.

- **Equitable Access:** Ensuring AI benefits all communities, not just those with resources, is crucial to reducing inequality.

2. Environmental Impact

- **Energy Consumption:** Training large AI models consumes vast amounts of energy, contributing to environmental degradation.

- **Sustainability Solutions:** Developing energy-efficient algorithms and using renewable energy sources for training AI models.

3. Philosophical Questions

- **Machine Autonomy:** As AI becomes more sophisticated, can it develop moral or ethical reasoning?

- **Human Identity:** What does it mean to be human in a world where machines can replicate creativity, decision-making, and empathy?

Conclusion: Balancing Innovation and Responsibility

AI's potential is boundless, but so are its ethical dilemmas. From bias and privacy concerns to misinformation and job displacement, addressing these challenges requires a collective effort from developers, governments, and society. By prioritizing transparency, fairness, and accountability, we can harness AI's power responsibly, ensuring it serves humanity as a force for good rather than harm. The choices we make today will define the ethical landscape of AI for generations to come.

6 FUTURE WORKFORCE

AI and the Future Workforce

Artificial intelligence is not only transforming industries but also redefining the skills and roles required to thrive in an AI-driven economy. As automation and AI systems take over routine tasks, the workforce must adapt to new realities. This chapter explores the skills, career opportunities, and collaborative dynamics shaping the future of work, offering insights into how individuals and organizations can stay ahead in an evolving job market.

Upskilling and Reskilling: Preparing for an AI-Driven World

The rise of AI is fundamentally shifting the skills in demand, emphasizing creativity, critical thinking, and technical proficiency.

1. Skills in Demand

- **Technical Skills:**

    - Proficiency in programming languages like Python, R, and JavaScript is increasingly valuable.

    - Understanding machine learning, data analysis, and cloud computing is essential for roles in AI development and integration.

- **Soft Skills:**

    - **Problem-Solving:** Complex decision-making and creative thinking remain uniquely human strengths.

    - **Emotional Intelligence:** As AI handles routine communication, interpersonal skills become critical for managing relationships and building trust.

- **Adaptability:** The ability to learn quickly and pivot in response to technological advancements is paramount.

2. Educational Programs and Initiatives

- **Upskilling Initiatives:**

  - Tech companies like Google and IBM offer free or affordable AI-focused certifications, such as Google's Career Certificates and IBM's AI Foundations.

  - Online platforms like Coursera and edX host courses in AI, machine learning, and data science from top universities.

- **Government Programs:**

  - Countries like Singapore and Germany invest in national reskilling programs to prepare their workforces for AI integration.

- o Public-private partnerships fund AI training initiatives for underserved communities.

- **Workplace Training:**

  - o Companies increasingly prioritize in-house training programs, ensuring employees can adapt to AI-driven workflows.

3. Lifelong Learning Culture

- **Mindset Shift:** The era of static careers is over. Workers must embrace continuous learning to remain relevant.

- **Accessible Resources:** The proliferation of online education democratizes learning, empowering individuals to upskill independently.

New Career Opportunities: Fields Emerging Due to AI

While AI may displace certain jobs, it also creates new opportunities in fields that didn't exist a decade ago.

1. Data Science and Machine Learning

- **Role Overview:** Data scientists and machine learning engineers develop algorithms, analyze data, and optimize AI systems.

- **Demand Surge:** The explosive growth of AI has made these roles some of the most sought-after in the tech industry.

2. AI Ethics and Policy

- **Role Overview:** AI ethicists and policymakers ensure that AI systems are fair, transparent, and aligned with societal values.

- **Emerging Field:** As AI's societal impact grows, so does the need for experts who can navigate ethical dilemmas and regulatory frameworks.

3. Robotics Engineering

- **Role Overview:** Robotics engineers design, build, and maintain AI-powered machines used in industries from healthcare to manufacturing.

- **Applications:** Robots powered by AI are increasingly critical in surgery, logistics, and exploration.

4. Human-AI Interaction Specialists

- **Role Overview:** These professionals focus on improving the usability and effectiveness of AI systems by enhancing how humans interact with them.

- **Future Demand:** As AI tools become mainstream, seamless user experiences will be paramount.

5. AI Trainers and Data Labelers

- **Role Overview:** AI systems require human-labeled data to learn. Trainers and labelers provide the annotations needed for models to improve.

- **Bridge Role:** These jobs often serve as entry points into more advanced AI careers.

6. Cybersecurity Specialists

- **Role Overview:** With AI automating many aspects of cybersecurity, specialists are needed to develop systems that defend against AI-driven threats.

- **Future Focus:** Addressing vulnerabilities in AI systems themselves is an emerging area of concern.

Collaboration Between Humans and AI

Rather than fully replacing humans, AI is increasingly seen as a tool to augment human capabilities. The future workforce will be defined by collaboration between AI systems and human workers.

1. AI as a Partner, Not a Competitor

- **Amplifying Productivity:** AI tools handle repetitive tasks, freeing humans to focus on higher-value activities like strategy and innovation.

- **Enhancing Creativity:** AI-powered tools like DALL-E and ChatGPT assist artists, writers, and designers, enabling faster and more diverse creative output.

2. AI in Decision-Making

- **Data-Driven Insights:** AI provides actionable insights by analyzing vast datasets, but humans remain essential for contextual interpretation.

- **Examples: In medicine**, AI suggests diagnoses while doctors make the final decisions. In business, AI forecasts trends while executives set strategic priorities.

3. Human Oversight and Accountability

- **Critical Role of Humans:** Workers will play an integral role in overseeing AI systems, ensuring their outputs align with ethical standards and organizational goals.

- **Collaborative Teams:** The workforce of the future will likely include hybrid teams of humans and AI, with distinct roles complementing each other.

4. Evolving Work Environments

- **Seamless Integration:** Technologies like augmented reality (AR) and AI-powered collaboration tools will redefine remote and hybrid work.

- **Example:** Virtual assistants that schedule meetings, summarize discussions, and automate follow-ups are becoming standard in digital workplaces.

Additional Considerations for the Future Workforce

1. Ethical Training

- Workers will need training in ethical AI use, ensuring they understand the societal implications of their tools and systems.

2. Regional Disparities

- **Challenges:** While some countries excel in AI adoption, others risk falling behind, exacerbating global inequalities.

- **Solutions:** International collaborations and knowledge-sharing initiatives can help bridge the gap.

3. Mental Health and AI Adoption

- **Adjusting to Change:** Rapid technological adoption can cause stress and anxiety among workers. Support systems will be vital to ensure well-being.

4. The Role of Unions

- **Unions may need to evolve to address challenges unique to AI-driven industries, such as negotiating retraining programs and ensuring equitable benefits for displaced workers.**

Conclusion: Embracing the AI-Driven Future

The rise of AI is not the end of work—it's the beginning of a new era where humans and machines collaborate to achieve unprecedented outcomes. Success in this future will require adaptability, a commitment to lifelong learning, and a willingness to embrace change. By investing in education, fostering collaboration, and addressing ethical concerns, society can ensure that AI drives progress while creating opportunities for all. The future workforce is one where humans and AI thrive together, complementing each other's strengths to build a better world.

7 REGULATION

Policy and Regulation: Navigating the Governance of AI

As artificial intelligence continues to evolve at breakneck speed, policymakers face the monumental task of regulating this transformative technology. The challenge lies in fostering innovation while safeguarding public interest, ensuring that AI develops responsibly, ethically, and inclusively. In this chapter, we examine existing legal frameworks, the pressing need for global standards, and the delicate balance between innovation and oversight.

Current Legal Frameworks: The State of AI Policy

AI governance varies widely across regions, with some nations taking proactive approaches while others lag behind. This uneven landscape reflects differing priorities, resources, and levels of technological development.

1. The United States: A Decentralized Approach

- **Current Landscape:**

  The U.S. adopts a sector-specific approach, relying on existing laws to regulate AI applications. For instance:

  - **Healthcare:** The FDA oversees AI-powered medical devices.

  - **Finance:** The SEC monitors AI in trading and fraud detection.

- **Key Initiatives:**

  - In 2021, the National Institute of Standards and Technology (NIST) released the AI Risk Management Framework to guide ethical AI development.

  - The Blueprint for an AI Bill of Rights (2022) outlines principles to protect individuals from AI misuse.

- **Challenges:**

  Fragmentation across sectors and states creates regulatory gaps, and rapid AI innovation often outpaces legislative efforts.

  ## 2. The European Union: A Leader in AI Ethics

- **The AI Act:**

  The EU's proposed AI Act is the first comprehensive attempt to regulate AI. It categorizes AI systems into risk levels—minimal, limited, high, and unacceptable—and imposes stricter requirements on high-risk applications (e.g., facial recognition, healthcare AI).

- **GDPR's Influence:**

  The EU's General Data Protection Regulation (GDPR) already sets a global benchmark for data privacy, influencing how AI systems handle personal information.

- **Ethics-First Approach:**

  The EU emphasizes ethical AI, mandating transparency, accountability, and fairness in AI deployment.

3. China: State-Driven AI Regulation

- **Strategic Goals:**

  China aims to dominate AI by 2030, blending aggressive innovation with tight government control.

- **Key Policies:**

  - Regulations target specific issues like deepfake content and algorithms that shape user behavior (e.g., recommendation engines).

  - The 2022 "Deep Synthesis Provisions" require labeling for AI-generated content.

- **Challenges:**

  While China's top-down approach enables swift policy implementation, concerns about surveillance and human rights loom large.

  ### 4. Emerging Markets:

- Nations like India and Brazil are developing AI policies tailored to local challenges, such as addressing educational disparities and healthcare access.

- Partnerships with global organizations and tech companies often play a key role in these regions.

The Need for Global Standards: Addressing Cross-Border Challenges

AI operates without regard for national boundaries, making international collaboration essential for effective governance. However, achieving consensus is no small feat.

1. The Cross-Border Nature of AI

- **Global Reach:**

  AI systems, such as social media algorithms and autonomous vehicles, impact users worldwide, requiring consistent standards.

- **Jurisdictional Conflicts:**

  Discrepancies between national regulations can create compliance challenges for multinational companies.

2. Collaborative Efforts to Date

- **OECD Principles on AI:**

  Adopted by 42 countries, these guidelines promote trustworthy AI development based on transparency, accountability, and fairness.

- **GPAI (Global Partnership on Artificial Intelligence):**
  A coalition of governments, academics, and industry leaders working to advance responsible AI practices.

- **United Nations Initiatives:**

  The UN advocates for global treaties addressing AI ethics and governance, focusing on equitable access and the prevention of misuse.

  ### 3. Barriers to Unified Standards

- **Geopolitical Rivalries:**

  Competition between AI powerhouses like the U.S. and China complicates efforts to establish shared rules.

- **Cultural and Ethical Differences:**

  Diverging views on privacy, free speech, and surveillance influence how countries approach AI regulation.

- **Pace of Innovation:**

  AI evolves faster than regulatory frameworks, leaving policymakers perpetually playing catch-up.

Balancing Innovation and Oversight:

A Delicate Dance

While regulation is essential, overly restrictive policies risk stifling creativity and hindering technological progress. The challenge lies in fostering innovation while mitigating risks.

1. Encouraging Innovation

- **Regulatory Sandboxes:**

  These controlled environments allow companies to test AI systems without the constraints of full regulatory compliance. For example, the UK's Financial Conduct Authority uses sandboxes to test AI in finance.

- **Incentives for Ethical AI:**

  Governments can offer grants, tax benefits, or recognition programs to encourage companies to prioritize responsible AI development.

- **Public-Private Partnerships:**

  Collaboration between tech companies and governments can spur innovation while ensuring compliance with ethical standards.

  ## 2. Addressing Risks

- **AI Safety Protocols:**

  Establishing clear guidelines for the development and deployment of high-risk AI systems (e.g., autonomous weapons, medical AI).

- **Algorithmic Transparency:**

  Requiring companies to disclose how their AI systems make decisions can build public trust and reduce biases.

- **Impact Assessments:**

  Mandating assessments to evaluate the societal, economic, and environmental impacts of AI before deployment.

3. Lessons from History

- **Internet Regulation:**

  Early missteps in internet governance highlight the need for proactive AI regulation to prevent unintended consequences, such as misinformation and monopolization.

- **Tech Adoption:**

  Balancing regulation and innovation in industries like biotechnology and aviation offers valuable insights for AI governance.

Emerging Areas in AI Regulation

1. Environmental Impact

- **Energy Consumption:**

  Training large AI models consumes significant energy, necessitating standards for energy efficiency and the use of renewable resources.

- **Sustainability Goals:**

  Policymakers can promote eco-friendly AI practices through incentives and penalties.

2. AI Accountability

- **Liability Frameworks:**

  Clear rules about who is responsible when AI systems fail—developers, operators, or users.

- **Auditing Requirements:**

  Regular third-party audits to ensure compliance with ethical standards and technical safety.

3. Global Equity

- **Access and Inclusion:**

  Policies must ensure that AI benefits all populations, addressing digital divides and resource disparities.

- **Knowledge Sharing:**

  International collaboration can provide developing countries with access to AI expertise and tools.

Conclusion:

Shaping the Future of AI Governance

The governance of AI is one of the defining challenges of our time. Striking the right balance between innovation and oversight requires collaboration among governments, industries, and civil society. While no single policy or framework can address all risks, a combination of flexible regulation, ethical guidelines, and global cooperation can create an ecosystem where AI thrives responsibly. As we navigate this complex landscape, the choices we make today will determine whether AI becomes a tool for progress or a source of harm.

7. The Future of AI

Artificial Intelligence (AI) is no longer a futuristic concept—it is here, evolving rapidly, and influencing every aspect of human life. But what lies ahead? This chapter explores bold predictions and transformative possibilities for AI's role in space exploration, climate science, and governance, the implications of achieving Artificial General Intelligence (AGI), and the power of human-AI collaboration to address the world's most pressing challenges.

Predictions and Possibilities: Transforming the World

AI's potential to revolutionize fields like space exploration, climate science, and societal governance offers a glimpse into an extraordinary future.

1. Space Exploration

AI is poised to become an essential partner in humanity's quest to explore the cosmos.

- **Autonomous Rovers and Satellites:** AI-powered rovers, like NASA's Perseverance, already analyze Martian terrain independently. Future iterations may explore moons, asteroids, or exoplanets without human oversight.

- **Interstellar Navigation:** Advanced AI systems can calculate optimal trajectories for spacecraft, enabling long-term missions beyond our solar system.

- **Search for Extraterrestrial Life:** AI can analyze massive datasets from telescopes and space probes, identifying anomalies that might signal alien life.

- **Space Colony Management:** In the future, AI could manage logistics and life-support systems for human settlements on the Moon or Mars.

2. Climate Science and Environmental Protection

AI holds promise in addressing one of humanity's greatest existential threats: climate change.

- **Predictive Climate Models:** AI systems can analyze decades of climate data to predict future weather patterns, helping governments and organizations prepare for disasters.

- **Carbon Capture Optimization:** AI can design more efficient technologies for capturing and storing CO_2, mitigating the effects of greenhouse gas emissions.

- **Wildlife and Ecosystem Protection:** AI-powered drones monitor endangered species and ecosystems, detecting threats like illegal logging or poaching.

- **Energy Efficiency:** Smart grids and AI-driven renewable energy management systems optimize energy consumption, reducing waste and reliance on fossil fuels.

3. Societal Governance

AI has the potential to make governments more efficient, transparent, and responsive.

- **Smart Cities:** AI can optimize urban planning, traffic management, and resource allocation, creating cities that are safer, greener, and more livable.

- **Data-Driven Policymaking:** Governments can use AI to analyze public data, identifying trends and crafting policies tailored to societal needs.

- **Justice System Enhancements:** AI could reduce judicial backlogs by assisting in legal research, case prioritization, and even mediating disputes.

- **Challenges:** Balancing efficiency with

fairness and avoiding bias in AI-driven governance will be critical.

The Road to Artificial General Intelligence (AGI)

AGI, the ability of machines to perform any intellectual task a human can, represents the next frontier in AI development. Its realization would fundamentally alter humanity's relationship with technology.

1. What Is AGI?

- **Defining AGI:** Unlike narrow AI systems designed for specific tasks (e.g., chatbots, image recognition), AGI would possess human-like reasoning, creativity, and adaptability across a broad range of activities.

2. Potential Benefits of AGI

- **Unparalleled Problem Solving:** AGI could tackle complex global issues like pandemics, poverty, and inequality with unprecedented efficiency.

- **Scientific Breakthroughs:** From curing diseases to understanding the origins of the universe, AGI could accelerate progress across scientific disciplines.

- **Economic Transformation:** AGI-driven automation could lead to an era of abundance, reducing costs and increasing productivity across industries.

3. Ethical and Existential Concerns

- **Control and Alignment:** How do we ensure AGI systems align with human values and priorities?

- **Job Market Disruption:** AGI's ability to outperform humans in most tasks could lead to widespread unemployment, necessitating a rethinking of economic models.

- **Potential Risks:** Unchecked AGI development could lead to unintended consequences, including the loss of human control over critical systems.

4. The Timeline for AGI

- **Optimistic Predictions:** Some researchers believe AGI could emerge within decades, while others caution that the challenges are far greater than anticipated.

- **Incremental Progress:** Breakthroughs in neural networks, quantum computing, and unsupervised learning bring us closer to AGI, but the road remains uncertain.

AI as a Partner in Innovation

One of AI's greatest strengths lies in its ability to collaborate with humans, amplifying creativity, efficiency, and problem-solving capacity.

1. Healthcare Partnerships

- **Drug Discovery:** AI algorithms analyze molecular data to identify potential drug candidates, a process that once took years but now takes months.

- **Personalized Treatment:** Doctors work alongside AI to tailor treatments based on genetic and lifestyle factors, improving patient outcomes.

2. Environmental Innovation

- **Agricultural Efficiency:** AI-powered tools help farmers optimize crop yields by analyzing soil conditions, weather patterns, and pest behavior.

- **Clean Energy:** AI collaborates with engineers to design more efficient wind turbines, solar panels, and energy storage systems.

3. Creative Collaborations

- **Art and Design:** AI systems like DALL-E generate unique visuals, while human artists refine and reinterpret them, pushing the boundaries of creativity.

- **Writing and Storytelling:** Writers use AI tools to brainstorm ideas, draft content, or generate dialogue, blending machine output with human storytelling.

4. Crisis Management

- **Disaster Response:** AI collaborates with emergency responders, analyzing real-time data to optimize rescue efforts and resource distribution.

- **Pandemic Preparedness:** AI systems assist researchers and policymakers in modeling disease spread, designing vaccines, and managing healthcare logistics.

Expanding the Discussion

1. The Democratization of AI

- As AI tools become more accessible, individuals and small businesses gain the ability to innovate on a level once reserved for tech giants.

- Open-source platforms and low-cost AI tools are empowering creators, entrepreneurs, and educators worldwide.

2. AI's Role in Cultural Preservation

- AI systems can digitize and analyze cultural artifacts, preserving endangered languages, traditions, and historical records for future generations.

3. Education in an AI-Driven World

- AI tutors and personalized learning systems ensure that individuals can upskill at their own pace, fostering a global culture of continuous learning.

Conclusion: Charting the Future of AI

The future of AI is boundless, filled with opportunities to revolutionize every aspect of human life. From space exploration to environmental preservation, the potential for AI to collaborate with humanity in solving our greatest challenges is unparalleled. However, this future also demands caution and responsibility, particularly as we edge closer to the possibility of Artificial General Intelligence. By fostering innovation, addressing ethical concerns, and ensuring global cooperation, we can shape a future where AI enhances human potential and leaves a legacy of progress, creativity, and equity for generations to come.

9 CASE STUDIES

Case Studies and Real-World Applications

Artificial intelligence (AI) is no longer just a futuristic concept—it is a powerful tool shaping industries and societies in real, tangible ways. By exploring both success stories and failures, we can uncover how AI is being leveraged to create value and the lessons learned from its missteps. This chapter dives into compelling case studies that illustrate AI's potential, as well as its pitfalls, offering insights into how we can harness this technology responsibly and effectively.

Success Stories: AI Transforming Industries

AI has enabled organizations to achieve remarkable breakthroughs, solving complex challenges and creating new opportunities. These success stories highlight how businesses, governments, and institutions are harnessing the power of AI for positive outcomes.

1. Healthcare: Early Detection of Diseases

- **Case Study: Google Health and Breast Cancer Detection**

    o Google Health developed an AI model capable of detecting breast cancer in mammograms with greater accuracy than radiologists.

    o **Impact:** Reduced false positives and missed diagnoses, enabling earlier intervention and better patient outcomes.

    o **Takeaway:** AI can enhance, not replace, human expertise, making healthcare more precise and accessible.

2. Finance: Fraud Detection at Scale

- **Case Study: PayPal**

    - PayPal employs AI algorithms to monitor millions of transactions daily, identifying fraudulent activity in real time.

    - **Impact:** Significant reduction in financial losses and improved customer trust.

    - **Takeaway:** AI's ability to process vast datasets and detect patterns is invaluable in combating fraud.

3. Agriculture: Maximizing Crop Yields

- **Case Study: Blue River Technology (Owned by John Deere)**

    - Blue River Technology uses AI-powered "see-and-spray" systems to identify and target weeds, reducing the need for herbicides.

    - **Impact:** Improved crop yields, lower environmental impact, and reduced costs for farmers.

- o **Takeaway:** AI-driven precision agriculture is transforming food production and sustainability.

4. **Retail: Personalized Customer Experiences**

- **Case Study: Amazon and Predictive Analytics**

  - o Amazon leverages AI to recommend products based on customer behavior, preferences, and purchase history.

  - o **Impact:** Increased sales, customer satisfaction, and loyalty.

  - o **Takeaway:** AI personalization can redefine customer experiences and boost revenue.

5. **Environmental Protection: Wildlife Monitoring**

- **Case Study: WWF and AI for Wildlife Conservation**

- The World Wildlife Fund (WWF) uses AI-powered drones and cameras to monitor endangered species and combat poaching in real time.

- **Impact:** Enhanced conservation efforts and protection of biodiversity hotspots.

- **Takeaway:** AI can be a critical ally in addressing environmental challenges.

Failures and Lessons Learned: AI Missteps and What They Teach Us

While AI has delivered remarkable successes, its implementation has also encountered significant challenges. These failures underscore the importance of transparency, ethical considerations, and robust testing.

1. **Bias in Recruitment Algorithms**

- **Case Study: Amazon's AI Recruitment Tool**

  - Amazon developed an AI tool to screen job applicants but discovered it was biased against women.

- o **Cause:** The algorithm was trained on historical data that reflected gender disparities in hiring.

- o **Outcome:** The tool was scrapped, sparking widespread discussions on algorithmic bias.

- o **Lesson Learned:** Data used to train AI must be diverse, inclusive, and free of historical biases.

2. Facial Recognition Controversies

- **Case Study: IBM and Law Enforcement Applications**

  - o IBM's facial recognition software faced criticism for inaccuracies in identifying people of color and its potential misuse by law enforcement.

  - o **Cause:** Biases in training data and the ethical implications of mass surveillance.

  - o **Outcome:** IBM halted its facial

recognition projects, advocating for responsible use of the technology.

- o **Lesson Learned:** Ethical considerations must guide the development and deployment of sensitive AI applications.

3. Chatbot Mishaps

- **Case Study: Microsoft's Tay**

  - o Microsoft launched an AI chatbot, Tay, designed to learn from Twitter interactions. Within 24 hours, it began spouting offensive and racist content.

  - o **Cause:** Tay's learning algorithm mimicked the inappropriate behavior of some users.

  - o **Outcome:** The chatbot was taken offline, and the incident highlighted the risks of unmoderated machine learning in public spaces.

  - o **Lesson Learned:** AI systems exposed to user-generated data require robust safeguards against abuse.

4. Autonomous Vehicle Accidents

- **Case Study: Uber's Self-Driving Car Program**

    - An Uber self-driving car struck and killed a pedestrian in Arizona, raising concerns about safety in autonomous vehicles.

    - **Cause:** The AI system failed to properly identify the pedestrian as a hazard.

    - **Outcome:** Uber paused its self-driving car tests, leading to a reevaluation of safety protocols.

    - **Lesson Learned:** Extensive testing in diverse scenarios is critical to ensuring AI safety.

5. Predictive Policing Pitfalls

- **Case Study: COMPAS and Criminal Sentencing**

    o The COMPAS algorithm, used in the U.S. criminal justice system, was found to disproportionately label Black defendants as high-risk for reoffending.

    o **Cause:** Bias in the historical data used to train the model.

    o **Outcome:** Public backlash prompted calls for greater transparency and accountability in AI-driven justice systems.

    o **Lesson Learned:** AI systems must be audited for fairness and subjected to ongoing oversight.

Emerging Themes from Case Studies

1. Transparency and Accountability

- Success: Companies like Google Health emphasize transparency in their AI projects, building trust and mitigating risks.
- Failure: Lack of transparency in cases like COMPAS eroded public confidence and highlighted systemic biases.

2. Ethical Oversight

- Success: Organizations that prioritize ethical AI, such as IBM, have taken bold steps to halt projects with potential for harm.

- Failure: The absence of ethical guidelines in chatbot experiments like Tay shows the dangers of ignoring ethical considerations.

3. Continuous Improvement

- AI implementations must be iterative, with lessons from failures guiding the next steps. Companies must be prepared to adapt and refine their systems based on real-world outcomes.

Expanding the Discussion: Additional Ideas for Case Studies

1. **AI in Disaster Management**

- **Example:** AI predicting hurricane paths and optimizing evacuation routes during natural disasters.

- **Outcome:** Saved lives and improved resource allocation.

2. **AI in Space Exploration**

- **Example:** AI assisting NASA's Mars rover in identifying geological formations of interest.

- **Outcome:** Accelerated discovery and more efficient exploration.

3. **AI in Art and Culture**

- **Example:** AI-generated music and visual art gaining acclaim but raising questions about authorship and creativity.

- **Outcome:** New avenues for artistic expression, but debates about intellectual property persist.

Learning from AI's Successes and Failures

AI's real-world applications showcase its immense potential to transform industries, solve global challenges, and improve lives. However, its failures remind us of the importance of ethical considerations, transparency, and rigorous testing. By studying these case studies, we can chart a course toward responsible AI development that maximizes its benefits while minimizing its risks. The future of AI depends on our ability to learn from the past, adapt to challenges, and embrace opportunities with caution and foresight.

10 CONCLUSION

Navigating the AI Revolution

The artificial intelligence (AI) revolution is no longer a distant possibility—it is here, shaping our present and defining our future. AI's dual nature as both a tool for immense progress and a potential source of risk presents humanity with one of its greatest challenges: how to harness this powerful technology responsibly. This conclusion reflects on AI's transformative potential, the responsibilities it places on individuals and societies, and the steps we must take to ensure AI enhances humanity's well-being rather than threatening it.

AI's Dual Nature: Progress or Peril?

AI's potential is boundless, but so are its risks. It is a technology that mirrors the values, intentions, and limitations of the people who create and deploy it.

1. A Tool for Progress

- **Medical Breakthroughs:** AI accelerates drug discovery, improves diagnostics, and personalizes treatments, saving lives and extending lifespan.

- **Climate Solutions:** From optimizing renewable energy to predicting environmental threats, AI is a crucial ally in combating climate change.

- **Global Connectivity:** AI bridges language barriers, enhances communication, and fosters understanding across cultures.

2. A Potential Threat

- **Erosion of Privacy:** AI-powered surveillance and data mining challenge fundamental rights to anonymity and personal freedom.

- **Job Displacement**: Automation threatens to disrupt industries, creating economic inequality and societal unrest.

- **Weaponization of AI:** Autonomous weapons and cyberattacks raise the specter of AI being used for destructive purposes.

3. The Choice Lies with Humanity

- Like any transformative technology, AI is neither inherently good nor bad—it is a reflection of how we choose to use it. Our ability to channel AI toward positive outcomes will determine whether it becomes a tool for progress or a source of peril.

Empowering Humanity Through AI

To ensure AI fulfills its promise of progress, we must act with intention, foresight, and ethical integrity. Empowering humanity through AI requires a commitment to equity, accountability, and collaboration.

1. Prioritizing Ethical Development

- **Transparency and Accountability**: AI systems must be auditable, explainable, and free from harmful biases. Clear accountability frameworks are essential to address failures or misuse.

- Inclusivity: Developers and policymakers must involve diverse voices, ensuring AI reflects a broad spectrum of human experiences and perspectives.
- **Ethical Guidelines:** Governments, organizations, and developers must adhere to ethical principles that prioritize human dignity and fairness.

2. Bridging the Digital Divide

- **Access for All:** Ensuring that AI tools and resources are accessible to underserved communities prevents the widening of economic and technological gaps.

- **Education and Literacy:** Investing in AI education for all levels—primary school to lifelong learning—equips individuals with the knowledge to navigate an AI-driven world.

3. Human-Centric Design

- **Enhancing, Not Replacing, Humans:** AI should complement human abilities, taking over repetitive tasks while leaving creativity, empathy, and decision-making to people.

- **Collaborative Systems:** Designing AI tools that work alongside humans fosters synergy and enhances productivity.

A Call to Action: Thinking Critically About AI's Role

The future of AI is not predetermined—it is shaped by the decisions we make today. This book aims to inspire readers to engage thoughtfully and critically with AI's role in their lives and the broader world.

1. Personal Responsibility

- **Understanding AI's Influence:** From personalized ads to social media algorithms, AI shapes our perceptions and choices. Recognizing this influence is the first step toward reclaiming agency.

- **Advocating for Responsible Use:** Individuals can demand transparency from companies and governments, ensuring AI is used ethically and equitably.

2. Community Engagement

- **Building Awareness:** Conversations about AI's impact should extend beyond tech circles to include educators, artists, policymakers, and everyday citizens.
- **Participating in Policy Discussions**: Civic engagement ensures that AI regulations reflect public values and address societal needs.

3. A Vision for the Future

- **A Shared Goal:** Imagine a world where AI powers breakthroughs in healthcare, combats climate change, and enhances education, while respecting privacy, dignity, and equity.

- **Sustained Vigilance:** Realizing this vision requires ongoing vigilance, adaptation, and collaboration as AI continues to evolve.

Expanding the Discussion: More Themes for the Conclusion

1. AI and Humanity's Identity

- **What Makes Us Human?** As AI becomes increasingly capable, it challenges traditional notions of creativity, intelligence, and individuality. How can we redefine humanity's role in an AI-driven world?

2. Preparing for AGI

- A Collective Effort: The potential arrival of Artificial General Intelligence (AGI) demands unprecedented levels of global collaboration to establish safeguards and shared goals.

3. Intergenerational Responsibility

- Building a Legacy: The choices we make about AI today will shape the world for generations to come. Acting responsibly now ensures a future where AI benefits all of humanity.

Final Thoughts

The AI revolution is an inflection point in human history. It holds the power to solve humanity's greatest challenges and create opportunities we have yet to imagine. But it also demands accountability, vigilance, and an unwavering commitment to ethical principles. This is not just the responsibility of tech companies or governments—it is a collective endeavor that requires the engagement of individuals, communities, and nations.

As we navigate this revolution, let us remember that the ultimate measure of AI's success will not be its sophistication, but its ability to enhance human life, uphold dignity, and foster a better world. The future of AI is in our hands—and the time to act is now.

ABOUT THE AUTHOR

Arthur Crandon is a retired lawyer and a prolific writer. He is British and grew up in a rural community in Somerset.

He has lived in England, Wales, Hong Kong and the Philippines and now spends most of his time in the Philippines with his Visayan wife and their son.

He loves to hear from anyone who has anything to do with the Philippines – you can email him anytime on:

ac@arthurcrandon.co.uk

The A.I. Revolution. Navigating the future of Artificial Intelligence

Copyright Arthur Crandon 2024

ISBN: 9798300518721

Cover design by Lynnie Ceniza

Interior design and formatting by Lynnie Ceniza

Published by Arthur Crandon Publishing

Visit our website: Arthurcrandon.co.uk

DISCLAIMER

The information provided in this book is for general informational purposes only. It does not constitute legal, financial, or professional advice. While every effort has been made to ensure accuracy, the author and publisher assume no responsibility for errors or omissions. Readers should consult with appropriate professionals for specific advice tailored to their individual circumstances.

First Edition: August 2024

If you enjoyed this book, please consider leaving a review – your feedback may help others to discover the book.

If you send me a screenshot of your review, I will send you a copy of another of my Self-Help books.

You can email me on
ac@arthurcrandon.co.uk